desire reclining

also by barbara cully

the new intimacy

desire reclining

barbara cully

penguin poets

PENGUIN BOOKS

Published by the Penguin Group
Penguin Group (USA) Inc., 375 Hudson Street,
New York, New York 10014, U.S.A.
Penguin Books Ltd, 80 Strand,
London WC2R 0RL, England
Penguin Books Australia Ltd, 250 Camberwell Road, Camberwell,
Victoria 3124, Australia
Penguin Books Canada Ltd, 10 Alcorn Avenue,
Toronto, Ontario, Canada M4V 3B2
Penguin Books India (P) Ltd, 11 Community Centre, Panchsheel Park,
New Delhi – 110 017, India
Penguin Books (N.Z.) Ltd, Cnr Rosedale and Airborne Roads, Albany,
Auckland, New Zealand
Penguin Books (South Africa) (Pty) Ltd, 24 Sturdee Avenue,
Rosebank, Johannesburg 2196, South Africa

Penguin Books Ltd, Registered Offices:
80 Strand, London WC2R 0RL, England

First published in Penguin Books 2003

10 9 8 7 6 5 4 3 2 1

LIBRARY OF CONGRESS CATALOGING-IN-PUBLICATION DATA

Cully, Barbara, 1955–
    Desire reclining / Barbara Cully.
      p. cm.
    ISBN 0-14-200343-3
    I. Title.
    PS3553.U337D47 2003
    811'.54—dc21   2003045619

Printed in the United States of America
Set in Electra
Designed by Sabrina Bowers

for my parents
John and Colleen Cully

and for
Frances Sjoberg

acknowledgments

I gratefully acknowledge the editors of the following publications in which these poems first appeared: *Sonora Review*: "Study of Death," "Meditation at Strahov"; *So to Speak*: "In Violet, Inviolate"; *POGTWO*: "Graveyard Soliloquy"; *Antennae*: "The Son She Expected No Longer Returns"; *Spork*: "Night Fishing," "Organizing a Piece of Cheese"; *Washington Square*: "Matters of Will"; *CUE*: "Coming to Meet."

My thanks to the dear friends who helped me at various stages of the writing of this book: Beth Alvarado, Victoria Garza, Richard Katrovas, Boyer Rickel, Frances Sjoberg—and especially Kim Westerman, without whose generous assistance the book would not exist in its present form. My gratitude to Cassie and Paul Youngborg and Katie and Roger Kingston who generously allowed me the use of their house on the Pacific Ocean at Playa la Misión, Baja California, Mexico, where I wrote many of these poems. Thank you is not enough to express the debt I owe to my parents, five siblings, and extended family: John and Colleen Cully; Patricia and Thomas Johnson; Joyce and Patrick Spencer; Kari, Steve, Stevie, and Sean Peacock; Kimberly and Kristine Adcox; John, Genevieve, Anthony, and Sophia Cully; Jacqueline Cully; Cully Clodfelter; and Cassie, Paul, Errol, and Nels Youngborg. Your gifts to me I return to the world modestly but earnestly. A delayed thank you to my teacher Dr. Alan Anderson, who years ago taught me the mysteries of reading the world as oracle by way of the *I Ching, or Book of Changes*.

Many thanks to Paul Slovak, editor; Maggie Payette, cover designer; Sabrina Bowers, book designer; and poets Carolyn Forché and Honor Moore who supported the manuscript before it was accepted for publication.

contents

desire reclining

in violet, inviolate

one

The beauty of the previous years now a solemn memory. What was honey-colored, what was spoken by chance but contained a porch and an hour. You, a leaping girl with illuminated eyes. Your father, also small, offering an entrée of stars. I heard that the leaves were destroyed because they wanted to live forever, that they threw away their usual caution for a commingling of hands and feet. I am sorry that I hurt you. The moon props awkwardly against the tide; the ocean too loud outside my window.

two

We know what killed the feline was not a miscalculation or a crisis of will. We know that to mortify is a transitive verb. There is no place to escape to. Ashes mark the footpath of the one who was hesitant or unguarded. In review, everything will have gone well until a single action makes a wasteland. In a box called The Devil's Country Favorites (other disgraces could occur to us), a forest grows freshly green after a fire.

three

Are the hills and mountains subject to spasms of perfectibility? Are they alive with remembered phrases and choral ecstasies resounding across a snow-lipped canyon on a waning New Year's Day? Steadfast, the mountain blunders into an act of keeping still when it is time to keep still. But it has trouble going forward when it is time to go forward. First we have desire in its box of solitude, a sheriff to seduction. Then the body with its hungers hoping to be tried. The penitent's punishment is ten million stones because duration in time is the image of all that is powerful.

four

The ocean is violet and orange at its edges. Dusk is the place to lie down and shrink effortlessly. Where we sit, a hummingbird has decided to take a rest: Luminous on a branch protected from the wind, provided the world does not end. Years ago in the maritime zone, more like lovers than friends, we gesticulated along the promenade. A brown spider worked at staying upright in dry sand. A battered mango flipped, rolling seaward in a wave rushing back.

five

Two versions of the end are at odds in the story of the snake and its god. Lose and go after that which is lost. No one can taste the darkness for you. Go naked in procession with your flaws and candles. Hang your harp on a willow. Now that you are captive, what is required is a song. After a long walk: Etched figures and red water lilies. Among the beach rubble enough evidence that the righteous worship a god of justice and anger. Wounded, we line up for our cupful. At the crucial moment the law will decree where to lay our heads: Harbor or willow, banishment or bondage.

six

Crossing the creek with the scorpion on its back, the frog is stung. Stinging, the scorpion knows the lack of beauty in the certainty of sinking. Mutually concerned with ethics, water, danger, and the vocabulary of instinctive behavior, their conversation lasted the length of the ride. They each would have preferred the other mark solemnly the spot where his own muddy toes or earlobes receded from sight. In an idyll where a few scattered hamlets make for a civility with dry patches, the continued forecast is overcast clearing by midday.

seven

The skin is stretched cleanly over muscle, organ, and bone. The eye in its cap, hidden from all but the unforeseen invasions. My old aunt falls from bed and slices her good eye on the chrome edge of her chair. We have heard the heroism of the ages rushing cleanly toward the baby tossed from the burning building. Your suffering days in the arroyos told me that when we die for love courageously (tragedy) we are not saved by the exercise of that courage. Tears (failing to honor) and remorse (what was ours or yours) are the armed forces of repentance and improvement, endlessly. On the scale of the Eternal Return. Do we avoid both by being on guard in time? Indeed, if time is the realm of gradual progress, I am certain we will meet again on the pier by the river.

eight

Nothing as pure or as clear as the soul, as they say. Nothing as uncompromised and unprofaned. In a morning of clipped vines and roses brought inward, I cock my ear windward. The high school girl raped repeatedly is told by her teacher that there is an emerald core that has not been touched. He opens a book of geological records and says, "Here—Here it is—See?" What I heard you say is that we go along thinking that what we are is inviolate. Until, when we ask for the count, we are called up short. You were wearing a sun-gold sweatshirt and offered me eggs. Not like Nadezhda Mandelstam offering Akhmatova the last egg in the house, sweeter. More like I woke up hungry and we were to go out.

meditation at strahov

one

At the Monastery at Strahov, the feeling of ocean, even from the tram and the distinctive scent of carnival on the air. Farewells: Farewell to the candy and to the flesh. I am here to reflect and to make my confession. There is a modicum of friendship in forgiveness. I am offering a pound of it. Here, take it, take it from me.

two

A triangular white stone not at all like snow, pyramidal, not at all like stone. On the third Sunday in ordinary time, dirtied gulls glorified the seaward climb. In the hermitage, the world's histories are free to announce themselves. West of darkness there was seen a great light, an abundant city later plowed to make way for a modern community, tumultuous and brilliant in the desert. From the museum's great height, there is a view clear to the shore. Off in the distance the stouthearted wait without nets, without fish, without courage. The citizenry even at its leisure is degraded. The leaders have not been careful; anguish has taken wing.

three

If you are a citizen of a forsaken land, if you commit an unsanctioned act, if you have not saved a holy book or a child, acceptable stories include the tale in which you turn to face fully the city everyone else in the story has successfully fled. It is in accordance with the rules that you are now made of salt or stone. You were asked only once to say which direction you were facing when the woman who loved you entered the room and walked slowly beyond the fire. It is good that all of your answers were true. It is in accordance with the rules that it is now your move.

four

We look out over the ancient views of bridges and kingdoms and offer prayers. When the words are whispered, and accepted, "I know my guilt. Nothing can remove it; nothing can allay my sadness for what I have done," there is the beginning of a permanent, earthly farewell. There is an historic solitude, a bowl of broth made with thrift and patience from a base of scrap and bones.

five

Perhaps emotion is more than the blood on the floor. I want to say, "It is wonderful, always, to hear from you; your messages always from far off with a tone of quietude ever near." Early spring, though today it is dark and rainy. With every blink the images of this place are more vivid than my home, the emptied desert with its brilliant sky. At one moment, the saddest, I stand behind a female figure. As I embrace her, she drops slowly into a plié out of my arms and steps to the right. Then she thinks better of it and tries to move back into my arms, but the musical phrase keeps going so she keeps going, moving past me again. All this is done slowly: We watch the music pull us apart.

six

A world is the impression left by the telling of a story. I remember the feeling of ocean up at the Monastery Strahov as we looked out over the city of Prague. The dance was not just frightening but comical, a pratfall. The weather moves from severe to sunny and the terrain from hardscrabble to lush. Knee deep in water, an ancient passage, crab-like up and down the beach.

———➤ ◄———

night fishing

one

As she wends through the canal leading into the bay, her boat passes under a small, arched bridge. She is alone, strong and slight, a bit of complexity passing over the stillness of the water. Tonight her friend will prepare something for her to eat and wait with it on the bridge. But as the hour approaches, the scene, suffused in the classical tradition of painterly composition, remains as it is. Left to resemble cave sketchings or sand art, time does not move. Hair slicked, shoes polished, the story remains steadfast, indifferent to the observer, needs in tow. The vignette is later described as *night fishing*.

two

We are attracted to every aspect of life that represents a last illusion yet unshattered. There comes a time when each action emblematic of a principle is graphically depicted in icons crafted for public consumption, a visual etymology a lot like ancient Chinese. The scroll reads best if it is understood as the musings of an outsider: On Tuesdays and Saturdays an unholy mixture of wheat and corn in discordant fields. On most any day, in a wind of pigeons or in complexity theory, the measure of information in a message is our inability to shorten it—tongue, tail, or wing.

three

Unusually high gates: But everyone knows that a scholar or the relative of a cardinal lives in the guest house. Songs and laughter, ducks in pairs, newly arrived swallows over the morning sand. Now and again vineyards at dusk, now and again at war. The rumor of a forsaken man drenched in sunlight, rain dripping from his shoulders. The important instant comes when he emerges in silhouette: A black figure risen from a ditch carved from the bog acres before he was born.

four

"Gone Fishing" reads the placard rusting in a desert window, fully inured to the heat. The more complete information is that everyone in the town is completely gone. One computation is that if a man hates his job and shows this in his gestures and speech and then the town's only factory is later torched, our man with the surly manners is the arsonist, more than 70 percent of the time. If we apply Master Bayes's mathematical theorem, we are able to compute minute probabilities in light of the statistical record and thereby avoid logical fallacies (or excuses). *The Book of Changes* on the other hand cautions the Marrying Maiden to consider her choices in the light of the eternity of the end.

five

Sometimes the scroll reads best as a bit of courtroom drama, a genre suited to the public formality of speaking and listening: Everyone dressed for their parts. The catch is, if you are unable to construct an acceptable narrative, you lose. The facts alone—all the detail you remember about the glass and the footprints regardless—the jury still holds perceptions of their own dearer than their curiosity about yours. Case number 366 (time out of mind): You are the driver in the familiar bus accident coming down to us across railroad lines: The town's children scattered, usually in the snow.

six

What is left of the family picture comes down whittled but saved, parched by the fire but soaked by the rescuer's hose. All of it cooling gradually like a volcano. The rosary from childhood, the rosary in your hands. The transistor radio muffled by your pillow while someone sings that his guitar gently weeps. Snow falls in the photograph. More snow etched on the surface in the pitch of survival and time. At the time of his death: The uncle in the middle of a painting depicting a brown bear rounding the corner of a cabin in the high desert woods. The cousin stopping his van to plant sunflower seeds in the marsh as the viper struck. Death or Satan, snake or fire, each day like any other day of summer. Morning sparrows and their rapid titters, afternoon shirtsleeves rendered superfluous by the blazing sun.

———————◆—————————

the son she expected no longer returns

one

Fire progresses by destroying the form of its fuel. It dissolves shapes, eliminates boundaries and, like water, breaks its captive down into his essential qualities. Bone is pulverized in the laboratory where the technician's possession of DNA is the same as holding a body. First the cell houses its story and then it begins to speak. The son on the eve of his birthday remembered in the yellowing dusk. In the maritime alley, under the bruised celestial dome, cypresses toss in a bestial heat.

two

When the Vatican's *Pietá* was taken to by a hammer, the Biblical and the contemporary suffering finally fused. The anguish formally presented by the statue now captured in the attempted destruction of the stone. The ability of marble to withstand its fate, and to represent ours, reclines in the form of Jesus and holds itself up in the form of Mary His mother safely behind glass. Across an expanse of tile, the polychrome confessional is as portable as the restorer's scaffold. We stand, we sing, we kneel. We promise to move heavenward in seven languages.

three

In the newspaper three rescued sons of the republic stand and weep. They sway in the arms of a man who has organized their fates as one sorts out silk threads from a knotted tangle and binds them into skeins. As in any mercenary period, the man wearing the expensive suit is a free agent; the men in uniforms are boys. The Doctors of Fortune, the opposing countries' chieftains, heighten their death fiestas: Computerized rocketry. Carefully applied cosmetics.

four

A grown man moves into the center of the lake eating bread with his parents. As seen from the shore. The storm foments its greenery, its funnel cloud, its earthly and unearthly desire. The water at its highest: The wave crest at its angle against the screech of a molting owl. The waiting and waiting. Something like the gnashing and the wailing.

five

In a box of luminous things: The last hour a mother spends washing the shirt of her son who was captured and flayed. When the shirt was sewn, it was dipped many times into the vat and hung many days on a line. Colorfast, what is left of the original yellow. What is lost is the mortal flesh unfurled, the boy aflame. Since there is no comfort to satiate her (the heavens fed), at the bottom of the box is the admonition to preserve her sorrow in a broth of laughter and a cake of songs.

———◆—◆———

study of death

one

When I heard you say, "Water escapes me yet marks me," you were sitting across from me blooming in a life's high season. In my office you were haunted by your blue dress, the image of it in the mirror across from you last week at the clinic. You talked about surviving the illness and your increased difficulties with the cure. A beautiful choice, blue, hanging empty across from you. Your exposed chest with its scar as a talisman. And your quietude as a protection into the end of the day. Always barely breathing, brave, you cleared your throat of everything before you spoke.

two

When I heard the news, I scattered. Out of the building onto the street, dismembered. Later on, on the beach, I would come across my limbs wandering each alone among the breakers. You slipped past me. You slipped under the conversation we were having into the eternity we talked about. Our literal feet resting on the floor and Whitman's "look for me under your boot soles" across the room. Across your forehead a curved spider dashed cleanly not announcing its escape.

three

In the Tomb of Hunting and Eating, stars float as fish: A plant has the appearance of a rope, a rope the appearance of a snake, and so on: Warriors, barefoot, pictured next to the Lady of the Beasts in a sacrifice scene: Noble women on horseback, intoxicated, the sacred and the profane interwoven with punishment and loss. In subsequent panels, we see these same women as attractive grotesques turning into wild boars or wolves.

four

Of course, at the shoreline's violent end, I will also fade. We will be everywhere seeking a god who walks between the buildings and who also rages. Later, after I live my life, I get to say, near me we were near the fire. You get to say, cross over; wither and fade; blossom to the sky. For a few it was the custom to go ashore when they found the madness overtaking them. Here I should mention the matter of the enormous waves. Those who were seized with the battle rage became beasts, and then they flung themselves against cliff sides and the huge rocks. At dusk, the low-light fire of the world, the water dragon, the poet puffing poppies then asleep in his cave of opium. The angels, losing no time, were putting something into what we were drinking, floral rosettes, fauns, the unaccounted for taste of truffles and women.

matters of will

one

A child lifts a bell with one hand and with the other leads a beast as unpredictable as a minotaur. The light principle is within. In evidence, the child's iridescent skin. The minotaur, mangy and cruel, stands upright and proves—genitals to throat—that the dark principle is without. In the hermitage. In the continuous present. High tide brings a sea lion ashore. A sparrow needles at the wings of the gull. In its way the day itself brings on the preponderance of the small.

two

Some participants maintain one attains significance by napping at the base of the stones. Our warrior with the bell fixes his eyes more closely on duty than the ordinary citizen. A whole life takes a shorter time than the trees pushing up the hill. Beast in check, snout to fin, he determines for himself what his duty is.

three

Through the crack of the door, songbirds then the familiar confusion between the nightingale and the lark. Before her lover flees, she places an outstretched arm and then her entire torso into the breach: Echoes of troubadours devoted to the codes of love. An alchemy of musty sheets. The scramble for a few minutes of a spring night. The overfunding of an expedition to insert the mirror as far as it will go. The body of the beloved lit like an entire pavilion. In the estuary egrets vie for the sweet grass designated for the horses: All love is forbidden love; all love loves a watershed.

four

The leaves of the quaking aspen, a stampede of dust muting the last of the summer's olives: He rode a horse so swift it left no footprints. Under him, she would lift her face to the sky. Near a field of sweeping fire, voices called: What might be that was? What could have been that was? Because they laid their eggs in the corpse of her soldier, the story goes, she welcomed the aphids to winter in her heart.

five

What it takes to move the body forward is called unworldly decisiveness. The fate of fire depends on fuel. If there is wood below, fire burns above. Already a ghost kneeling beside the lake, he offers the lily in his right hand to be able to do what his orders demand.

———————▸ ◂———————

organizing a piece of cheese

one

On New Year's Day the same ram's horn trumpet that shall be blown on Judgment Day. I walk the stone shoreline to the base of the bloodied wall. What does the Lord require of me? To do justly, to love mercy, to walk humbly. And, if I listen carefully, my own flesh as a burnt offering. If I push my cart through the thorn thicket when the rain flood falls from the open sky, if I push my cart up the slope of the ravenous wolves—if I let eight days pass—is it the darkness or the Almighty that cuts me off from the table of my friends?

two

Who was it who promised to prepare a feast in the presence of the enemies? The horror strikes at the peak of the century, dark already come. The lame girl walks into dusk not knowing how long it takes a survivor. The Lord is your shepherd, but in the green night it is time to become a predator, to organize daily a simple egg or a piece of cheese. In the dense night murderers pass the gate. In the ebony night whole households are buried near the river.

three

A remote fire breaks out on the plain. Eagles and jets fly into the flames in a Ferris wheel of folly and strength. As prophesied, fallen angels lie scattered like downed pelicans on the mute palate of the strand. From time to time heroes enter the story so subtly you'd think they were fish or stones. Actual stones glitter weakly in the bridge over the lagoon. The caped hermit contemplates the weather laid like dinner before him: Deep disappointment with the thickening clouds despite a certain fullness. Deep disappointment with their violet reds and pleasures.

four

Do not be afraid: As a certain warning the snake and the sunflower will be as gold as they are ever allowed to be when the world, unpredictable as it promises to be, comes to an end a second time. Then, simply, we will heed the signs: The bee circling in the clover and the wine maker mending his shimmering vines. When it happens, my friends will be the women under the umbrellas in the field, and surely I will be the drunkard running and waving to them with a lilac kite. I'll call to them as the final boat circles the edge of our glorious island, and we will be among those expecting the second round of pillage, fireworks, and thunder. Or, we will heed the violin of our darkness and assure all the scarred and earthly dead that there will be no other end.

in a time of scanty resources

one

At the foot of the mountain, the lake
At spontaneous affection, the transitory
At the cloud height, the gull
At the water's break, the ruin
At the ruin, the end
At the end, the light of eternity

two

Two figures, opposing but huddled, next to the roar of snow wash. Boulders gray in the distance and gray and cold so near. Upward, they see five hawks circling and, for a moment, an octagonal tower and a sudden terrace or roof deck, gold at end of day. Their conversation in this wild remains cylindrical and unmoving, a building in winter exactly square. Precisely unreachable from any side, on a grassy plinth, the edifice disguised as idyllic love wears its double-banded cornice as a crown.

three

Lying to either side of the grass, the gravel edges the exterior wall and borders the graves. A soaring entry canopy pierces the church as a relief of molded glass. The worshipers, on tour, are led through the vestibule and the bay across acres of geometric tile: This fortified box with its air well like a threshold, with its eaves as songbirds peeling upward in a parapet. Looking skyward through folded planes, the funnel effect, like a flirt: All conjured to convince us of the structure's mystery or its maker's power.

four

What demons pursue us, what hauntings we trail
What blessings we produce for one another here
Will be recorded for the heart song and the tear
The valley at the edge of the notebook
The seamless water, its crab and whale

five

In a time of scanty resources, the myth of plenty mocks the rubber sandals held over a second summer. I turned from my companion and more fallen each time ran tumbling along the sea rocks and coal. Regret, a solid bed, my voice and tongue creeping from me like a snake among the tombs. At four-fifty in the afternoon, olive trees twist in benevolence. Friends who have not been friends dine on a honey-glazed patio before an enormous fire. The pounding heart, the drooping mouth, the eyelid wrinkled in a place neither wet nor dry, neither singular nor plural.

six

In every instance of tenderness or calamity, forgiveness is in the hands. At the crossroads the accused are either gathered in a solemn mass or allowed into a clearing: A cool, mid-autumnal rotunda, a place to reconnoiter the death and the dawn of it—the fish and the fowl, the fool and the fair—all that lies in the history of your heart equally real.

———→ ←———

coming to meet

one

I knew I would write to you, despite the appalling forecast: 103 through Wednesday. (This isn't my ocean exactly.) I knew we would resume our trek and the telling of a story, assuming that a world is the impression left by the telling. The hike down, when it *is* down, always makes the legs shaky even when they are not weak, in that every step makes for a distracting background meditation on the way back up. Then there's the listening, itself raised to an art. You told me to use you in any way I want. It surprises me each time I know that I have. You catch me wanting to apologize. Something about my eyes surfacing when the sun reasserts itself over the canyon wall. Not walls exactly, a cascading of creamy boulders and scrub oak only squirrels navigate expertly, free of our instinctual caring about which end is up. If we come to rest, if we go ahead and recline in the middle of the trail, the two figures visible in the distance might walk right over us. Or, at the correct moment we will rise to greet them as we would our lovers coming to meet us. As we dust ourselves off, it occurs that the first order of business in movement of any kind is to determine direction: From where to where.

two

And the second decision is about the movement's speed. I wanted something more relaxed and conversational, a stormy morning interspersed with steady altos. A repressed theme cresting in the testimony of a spirited witness who only later comes to have an unquestioned stake. Something about the jaw muscles that allows the face to relax into song or reverie, in the front seat of a car. The habit or gait that allows for an easy ambulatory writing of a letter. Cutting the sentences in the way thoughts break off mid-finish as when talking to a workmate or a friend. We are nearing the largest canyon when the western horizon throws all of its scarlet across the eastern walls. As a I turn to silhouette—my head and its contents hooded, my face cresting—you are there to remind me it's OK if our advance toward one another halts mid-flourish. As long as it is modulated, this journey, there will be time for peripheral rustlings. Tiny desert creatures to distract us from a sense of destination and distance from ourselves.

three

Along the way, noted but not spoken: Short sequences that change abruptly. At one point, a figure on the trail who has been caterwauling alone is confronted by a lineup of spirits—the fates, the graces, the wives, we never find out. A longish dramatic history fills each caesura with urgency. A doubt whether the scene is going to develop forces us to listen more sharply. Because the desertscape is not flowing into the skyline in exactly the way expected, we actually see stars. We see a scarecrow riveted as he faces the jury of women. We see their three handsome jawlines like mountain ridges all in a row. We see his shrunken body in its effort, its pathos. And loss, loss is there, that old chestnut with its face made up again shoved back into the light.

four

What remains in the open air becomes eventually soaked, becomes in this riparian setting (twigs and hair) all photography—all done with light and décor—what the eye via its sensors hungers to record. What the voyeur does not actually see, monster, he eats. Not the person but her movement across a surface. Not the distance but a volcanic plateau. Forest to ash puffing, the body's stride as repetition. Two figures coming to meet as a length of time in seconds. Not private but regarded as from above in a distant surveillance. A letter read and restated. As a refrain repeated.

five

The utilitarian philosopher asks us to look at history and to count—quantity of life takes precedence—the copious beauty of the cows over the singular beauty of the damaged children. In the luminous eons ants lug their tremendous weight onto the highway. Dry turtles appear from nowhere and drive next to us along stony ridges in the rain. In the appalling distance, my demons appear as disassociations from my own muscles, lips and tongue as inert as rock or bone. A couple of mourning doves settle next to a few figs tethered. OK. A new day. Slips of unread paper in a new wind roaring.

six

Since the loss of our friend, I have gathered my strength greedily as wildflowers from grief to grief. But I want to bring the story back down gently, back to what is happening "on the ground," as they say. I haven't often encountered evil, almost never. Rather, amid forces beyond my control, I allowed hungers within it to rise. Is this the noon hawk that mutilates before it dines then soars, its aftermath the scorched bleat shivering? Are we or is the heart we did not put first the fallen horse that leads the way away? Blood bonds and transparencies: *Yes, I loved her.* Cloud beyond the light. As the poet said, dark things tend to brightness. I offered my hand, dark thing. I offered my heart darker still.

seven

When talking about intimacy and its primal scene, if you ask, as about a dance, for the number of figures involved in the action, you might as well consult Vienna. Eight or nine at least. Enough to want to have it catered. Those in the farthest rows will want to know, Did the actors end the action on or off the stage? On. They started it off and ended it on. No one saw them approach one another, come to meet, embrace, traverse a distance— and more—and go away. Once backlit by moonlight—the buildings far behind—they set their instruments to the lowest range.

———➤ ◄———

graveyard soliloquy

one

Not in search of the sun only. In search of the plain. The whitewashed chapel, roots and the branches of roots, the foot of the *santo* seated thus. A figure seen in the last stage of making before the polishing. Closer examination reveals the right eye is imperfectly carved. The supine queen composed of thirteen blocks. Then the addition of four, measured along the variegated thigh. What can be seen, what can be written or drawn, can also be wiped away, perhaps a number of times. Her understated desire, the stark white contour of the stone enhancing the eyes. Your own desire, a wooden drawing board of the kind used by workers or students. There is clear indication that the surface has been marked with red highlights in a grid, clear indication that erasures have been made on this board.

two

Dead that bend their fingers dark around a stone. The living that bend their fingers thus. O, what door is shut? O, the lupine and the wisteria creeping. The opportunity to listen much the same as the opportunity to be good. Animals in relief, and writing, dogs and swans, brass roses in an endless cascade. A brisk rendition of poppies in September, silt in summer, washed until only the mountain remains. Hymnless, I have broken herbs into a glass to make someone laugh. No, I have broken a promise to make someone tea.

three

From famine to your own land, from prehistory to a documentary manner,
debris and grave finds in bronze and amber.
Fruit and salt, the explorer's hunger for pith and loam,
a child mummified in a heap of bark and stones.
The river's bear, the river's bottle, the river's campsite broken.
What we heard in the caution to preserve the dear and gone,
withered bodies that speak loud and long.

four

In the Last Judgment you've been implicated in a mosaic of unclothed servants in an unchecked bathing scene. Your own hunger lists in the courtroom to the side of the damned. Many a mulberry and many a spring, clay or bread, substance or steam, before baking, your torso soft against a granite queen.

five

What is in you is called form; what it makes of you is called desire. When your adversary is stronger than you, it is not advisable to push conflict to the point of blood or a decision. Better to be like water which flows into the form that contains it, yet breaks through all containers, filling up every empty space before moving on.

———● ◆———

coming to rest

one

When we finally come to rest, the flagrant butterfly and the concealed snake recede from view. The acolyte receives a sacred thread from the teacher. Soon the disappearance of the granite of the mountains and then the mountains themselves. In direct sunlight, impossible to develop: A philosophy that excludes the dark blue bee and the iridescent parrot with red eyes. High above the waves, a formation of pelicans turns the sky as expertly as a pilot commandeers a fire. Amid the day's destructions, no accounting of creation that omits tomato worms igniting spontaneously or seahorses pumping babies into the open sea.

two

The entrance to the port, placid by water, by land is a spectacle. The old highway swings down the mountain grade and crosses a little valley below the lighthouse. From there it works its way along the ridge between the ocean and the high half-vertical hills and follows the narrowing passage until blocked by a massive cinder. As good a place as any to spend the winter. From the height of the bridge, you could prove that the silver strand is an island or that the slate mass carving a dome in the foggy sky is no island at all.

three

It is possible to drift and still see the mustard on the hills lit by a hazy sun. The visage of the day assembles like a carnival mask that can be held up for protection like a painted fan. On it a warrior stands in readiness fully exposed to typhoon winds and departures that begin on the waterfront. On the opposite side, the warrior faces an alluring half-moon bay dotted with pleasure craft left at anchor.

four

In the inner sanctum, at every turn, a shrine to receiving the world as purely as we can. In the gallery of 330 million divinities (a mammalian and humanoid cast), every stage of thinking about the past: Cause or causes, available materials, catalogues of color and form. In a wilderness of honeycomb crumbling gradually into wheat grass and wildflowers: Cottonwoods tremulous in the slight movement of the hour. Inside the monks' memorial: Skeletons laid as lovingly as bridal sheets. Their notice above the threshold reads: Salvation is as near to you as your hands and feet.

five

In friendship the only rupture is betrayal, the first consequence a lurching of the untidy script and set. The players, good as they are at their instruments, are not prepared to suffer. When it happens, a muddy-wheeled cart tilts jagged between the palm trees' wide rows just where the narrow track cuts off from the main road. No, what seems distant here (the ocean) is very near and what seems near (the rising tide) is very far away. I mean, bicycle and rider and a small cart, used now as they are as rafts, careening until those who once sang together watch a darkening sky surround a single horse. Deep furrows fissure and clay lumps shatter until everywhere horse and rider are buried by good fortunes dwelling in a rear view suddenly—

six

Dark paintings on the water. The point of retreat is to leave behind the clamor of the world, to stoop long enough to hail an insect and to taste God. Every day the forecast calls for night and morning low clouds continuing into an orange and violet dusk. There the major high tide blesses the inhabitants of every home with a gold crescent they, and their neighbors, call the moon.

———➤ ◄———

notes

"In Violet, Inviolate": Sections one and two borrow from Rafael Alberti. Section three alters a passage in the *I Ching, or Book of Changes*.

"Meditation at Strahov": Section five owes a debt to Joan Acocella. The first sentence in section six is from the *Yogavasistha*.

"Night Fishing": The first statement of section two condenses a sentence in Marcel Proust's *Remembrance of Things Past*.

"The Son She Expected No Longer Returns": The title refers to Constantine Cavafy's "Supplication." The first sentence in section one and the simile in section three are from the *I Ching*.

"Study of Death" is for Sylvia Sohn Um.

"Matters of Will": The last sentence of section four alters a passage by Hsu Chao.

"Organizing a Piece of Cheese": The poem is influenced by Johannes Bobrowski and Czeslaw Milosz. The third and fourth sentences of section one paraphrase Micah, 6:8 in the Torah.

"In a Time of Scanty Resources": The title and phrases in section one are borrowed from the *I Ching*. Section five echoes lines of Rafael Alberti and Aleksander Wat.

"Coming to Meet": The poet in section six is Eugenio Montale.

"Graveyard Soliloquy": Section five closes with an idea from the *I Ching*.

"Coming to Rest": Section five borrows from a poem by Sandor Weores.

about the author

Barbara Cully is the author of *The New Intimacy* (Penguin, 1997), which won the National Poetry Series Open Competition, and *Shoreline Series* (Kore Press, 1997). She has received fellowships from the Arizona Commission on the Arts and has been Writer-in-Residence for the YMCA Writer's Voice. She has taught at the Prague Summer Writers' Program and currently teaches in the Department of English at the University of Arizona.

Penguin Poets